E220181194

C000245272

# LIFE CYCLE OF A
# BUTTERFLY

By Kirsty Holmes

Words that look like **this** can be found in the glossary on page 24.

©2018
Book Life
King's Lynn
Norfolk PE30 4LS

**Written by:**
Kirsty Holmes

**Edited by:**
Holly Duhig and Imogen Ramsdale

**Designed by:**
Daniel Scase

**ISBN:** 978-1-78637-282-6

A catalogue record for this book is available from the British Library.

## PHOTO CREDITS

# LIFE CYCLE OF A
# BUTTERFLY

# WHAT IS A LIFE CYCLE?

All living things have a life cycle. They are all born, they all grow bigger, and their bodies change.

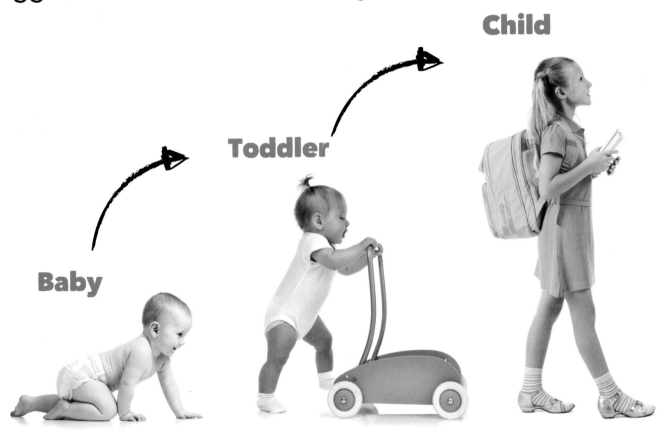

**Child**

**Toddler**

**Baby**

When they are fully grown, they have **offspring** of their own. In the end, all living things die. This is the life cycle.

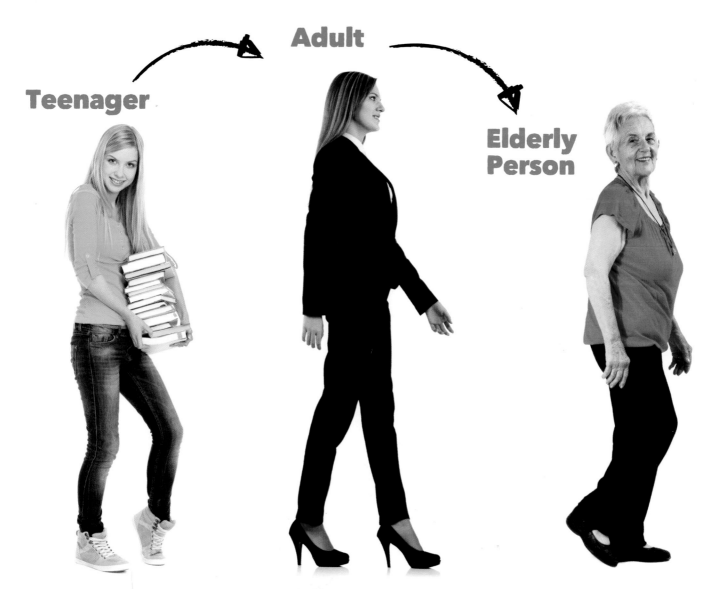

Teenager

Adult

Elderly Person

# BEAUTIFUL BUTTERFLIES

Butterflies are flying insects. They have four large, scaly wings which can look very beautiful. They have six legs, and a special long feeding tube, called a proboscis.

Butterflies can 'smell' the air with their **antennae**!

Wings

Antennae

Proboscis

Butterflies are very good at flying. Some fly very fast, and others fly very slowly. They suck **nectar** from flowers, or juice from fruit, using their long proboscis.

Butterflies can live all over the world, but most like warm weather.

# EXCELLENT EGGS

The eggs are stuck to the leaf using super-sticky glue made by the female.

Female butterflies lay eggs. The female will look for a safe spot, near to some food, to lay her eggs. She will lay lots and lots of them.

Inside each egg, a baby butterfly – called a larva – grows. When it is time to hatch, the larva chews its way out of the shell, which it then eats for a first meal!

Butterfly eggs come in lots of different colours and shapes.

Monarch Caterpillar

# CURIOUS CATERPILLARS

When the larva has hatched, it is called a caterpillar. Caterpillars eat, and eat, and eat!

Some caterpillars eat leaves. Others eat grass, flowers or **bark**.

Caterpillars have a hard outer layer called an **exoskeleton**. Because caterpillars grow so fast, they have to wriggle out of this layer when it gets too small, and grow a new one. This is called moulting.

Caterpillars moult four or five times because they grow amazingly fast!

# THE CREATIVE CHRYSALIS

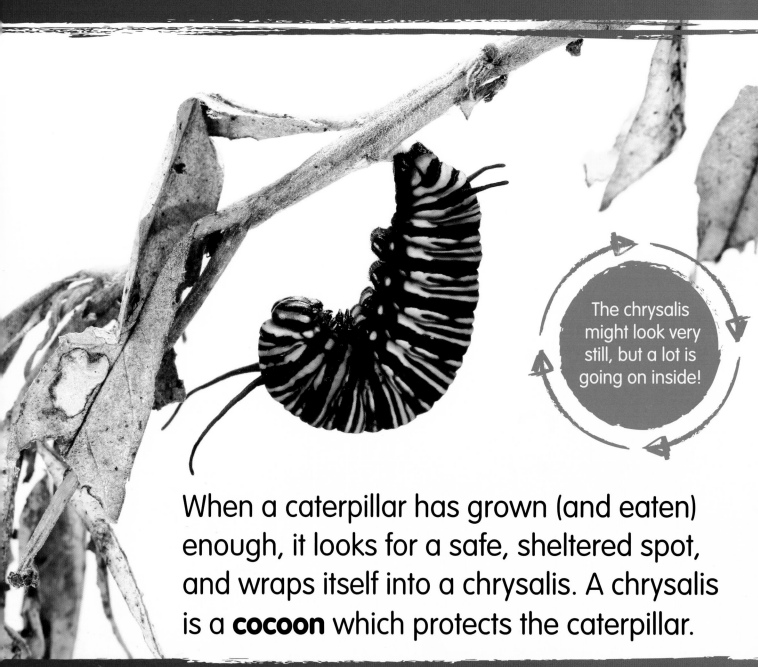

The chrysalis might look very still, but a lot is going on inside!

When a caterpillar has grown (and eaten) enough, it looks for a safe, sheltered spot, and wraps itself into a chrysalis. A chrysalis is a **cocoon** which protects the caterpillar.

Inside the chrysalis, the caterpillar moults one last time and becomes a pupa. The pupa stays in the chrysalis for up to two weeks.

The pupa forms wings, legs, antennae and a proboscis inside the chrysalis.

# BRILLIANT BUTTERFLIES

The special change that happens in the chrysalis is called 'metamorphosis'. When it is ready, the chrysalis becomes see-through and then the new butterfly hatches!

Leopard Lacewing Butterfly

When the butterfly first hatches, its wings will be soft and folded up. By the time it is three to four hours old, the butterfly will be able to spread its wings and fly.

# LIFE AS A BUTTERFLY

Adult butterflies spend their lives looking for food and a **mate** so they can produce their own offspring.

Butterflies like to rest and enjoy the sunshine. They don't like to fly in the rain.

Some butterflies **migrate** to find warmer weather if it gets too cold.

# FUN FACTS ABOUT BUTTERFLIES

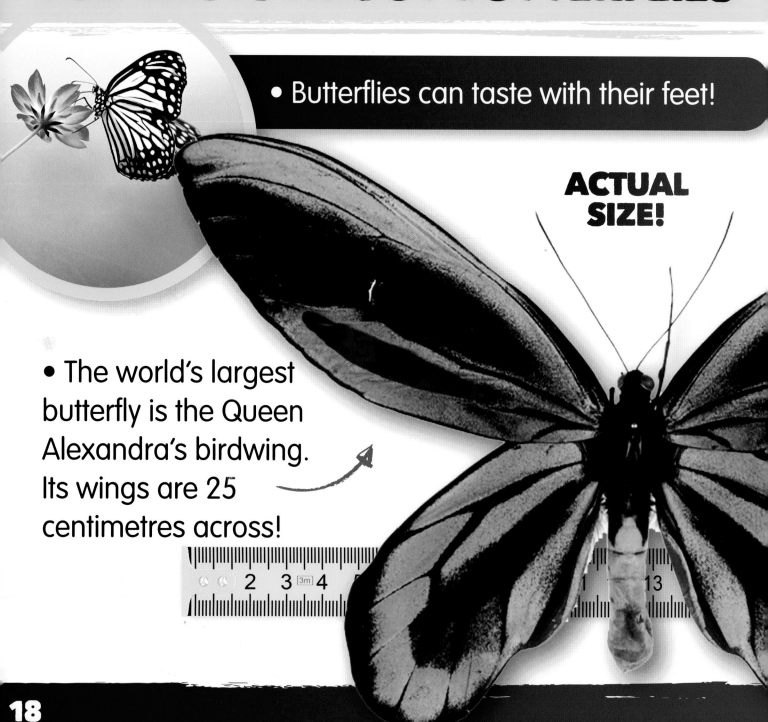

• Butterflies can taste with their feet!

**ACTUAL SIZE!**

• The world's largest butterfly is the Queen Alexandra's birdwing. Its wings are 25 centimetres across!

- There are between 15,000 and 165,000 different types of butterfly.

- A group of butterflies is sometimes called a 'flutter'.

- The smallest butterfly is the western pygmy blue. Its wings are only 12 millimetres across.

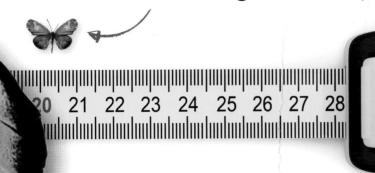

20 21 22 23 24 25 26 27 28

# THE END OF LIFE AS A BUTTERFLY

Most butterflies live for a few weeks, but some **species** can live for up to nine months, especially bigger butterflies.

Most butterflies die after they have mated and laid their eggs.

Butterflies also have lots of **predators** to watch out for. Wasps, birds, snakes, toads, rats, lizards, spiders and praying mantises all eat butterflies.

# THE LIFE CYCLE

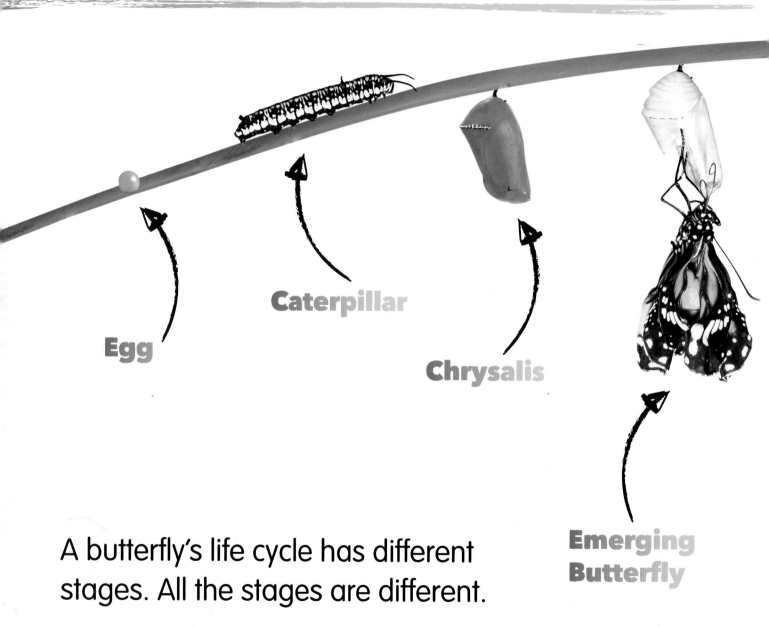

Egg

Caterpillar

Chrysalis

Emerging Butterfly

A butterfly's life cycle has different stages. All the stages are different.

Fully Emerged Butterfly

Adult Butterfly

In the end, the butterfly dies, and the life cycle is complete.

The butterfly egg hatches into a caterpillar. The caterpillar makes a chrysalis and changes into an adult through metamorphosis. The adult butterfly has offspring.

# GLOSSARY

| | |
|---|---|
| **antennae** | a pair of long, thin sensors found on the heads of insects |
| **bark** | the outside cover of the trunks, branches, and roots of woody plants |
| **cocoon** | a silky case spun by the larvae of many insects for protection as they change into their adult form |
| **exoskeleton** | a hard structure on the outside of a creature |
| **mate** | a partner (of the same species) that an animal chooses to produce young with |
| **migrate** | the seasonal movement of animals from one area to another |
| **nectar** | a sweet liquid made by flowers in order to attract insects |
| **offspring** | the child or young of a living thing |
| **predators** | animals that hunt other animals for food |
| **species** | a group of very similar animals or plants that are capable of producing young together |

# INDEX